# Visa to Paradise	28 de septiembre ## 2011	
To live in Cuenca Ecuador You do not have to do much, just pack your bags and go.		Living in Cuenc a

Cuenca

Why Cuenca?

1.-A retirement program that will save you thousands of dollars a year.

2.-A U.S.-dollar-based economy

3.-Affordable private health insurance plans and a new *free* government health plan that expat residents can take advantage of.

4.-Perfect weather year-round

5.-Top-notch medical care at one-fourth to *one-tenth* the costs of the U.S.

6.-The *lowest* cost of living. (Other expat reports monthly expenses <u>as low as $500</u>!

Cost of Living

Electricity	$50
Water	$8
Gas	$3
Telephone	$5
DirecTV	$75

Internet	$50 or less.
Groceries	$350 (includes wine)
Transportation	$25 (buses and taxis)
Entertainment	$50
Condo dues	$100
Ecuador IESS health plan	$53
Others	$100
Total	**$ 869**

Cuenca is the third most populous city in Ecuador, after Guayaquil and Quito, with 329,928 inhabitants in the urban administrative area, in real data of urban agglomeration in the suburban areas including rural headers already merged with the town: Baños, Ricaurte, San Joaquin, Turi and Sayausi determine the actual population of the city of Cuenca with 385,456 inhabitants. Also worth mentioning that the county as a whole has 505,585 inhabitants. All these data according to the latest census conducted on November

28 2010 being the urban area has the largest number of inhabitants. That is due in part to the increase in available jobs and housing.

The city was declared Cultural Patrimony of Humanity by UNESCO on December 1, 1999 and in the center of town there are important historical ruins, museums and old churches (such as the Cathedral of the Immaculate Conception, one of the largest and America Beautiful, and others dating from the XVI and XVII), cobbled streets and houses with facades Republican who point out the various European influences with characteristic balconies and carved ceilings and other artistically painted forged brass.

The city is also known as the "Cuenca de los Andes" or the "Athens of Ecuador" for being the birthplace of poets and illustrious men who have made up the name of this city, as Miguel Velez, Gaspar Sangurima, Santo Hermano Miguel Honorato Vazquez, Remigio Crespo Toral, Jose Peralta (Canar), among other characters like Garaicoa Abdon Calderon, Antonio Borrero. In Cuenca, there are numerous cultural organizations.

Visas and Residency in Ecuador

Becoming a Resident

It is recommend that you hire an Ecuadorian immigration attorney to help you navigate the visa process. Contact your attorney for the latest.

Staying on a Tourist Entry

When you first enter Ecuador, you will receive a T-3 tourist stamp in your passport, allowing you to stay in the country for 90 days.

If you wish to stay more than 90 days within a year, go to an Ecuador consulate in your home country and apply for the 12-IX visa. Often referred to as the Tourist, Commercial or Sports Visa, this allows you to stay in the country for up to 180 days in a year. If you are planning to apply for permanent residency, you are required to have the 12-IX visa when you file your application.

Why Get a Resident Visa?

While both non-resident and tourist visas can keep you in the country for a while, only the resident visa will allow importation of your goods duty free. Also, the tourist visas given upon entry have cumulative time limits per calendar year that cannot be reset by leaving and entering the country. Resident visas can be obtained while in Ecuador on a tourist visa, but the process can be much simpler at consulate back home if you're doing it yourself.

If you're using an attorney, the process is even easier, and they can deliver your visa to you here in Ecuador, or have it sent to you in your home country (via the consulate) before you depart.

Absences From the Country

The resident visas outlined below will grant you permanent residency. That means you'll be allowed to come and go from Ecuador as you wish. However, you can't be absent from the country for more than 90 days per year during the first two years of your residency, nor more than 18 consecutive months after your second year of residency.

Varieties of Resident Visas

9-I: Pensioner Visa

This visa is intended for retired persons who receive pensions from their native countries (pension from a stable source, at least $800 per month). Also for an annuity recipient or trustee who will live on cash deposited in the Central Bank of Ecuador or on income from a trust. In the case of a deposit or trust, the amount must be that which would result by multiplying the monthly minimum over a period of five years.

This amount may vary from $800 monthly and will be determined by the Immigration Advisory Board.

9-II: Investor of Real Estate or Securities Visa

This is for real estate and securities investors who are investing at least $25,000.

9-III: Industrial Investor Visa

For investors in industry or investors who wish to export agricultural products, livestock, or minerals, provided they bring capital the equivalent of at least $30,000.

9-IV: Legal Representative, Work Visa, or Religious Visa

Intended for foreign local agents who possess unlimited power of attorney to represent a company in Ecuador, provided that 80% of the company's local personnel are Ecuadorian. Also technicians or technical experts under indefinite work contract with a company established in Ecuador, and members of religious organizations. (An indefinite work contract is one that does not have a specified term.)

9-V: Professional Visa

For professionals with university degrees recognized by a national university who wish to practice their profession in Ecuador. Should the applicant's profession not exist in Ecuador, the degree must be locally certified. The applicant must also fulfill the Ecuadorian requirements for such practice, such as bar exams, etc.

9-VI: Economic Dependence Visa

This is for individuals economically dependent on a spouse or a blood-related family member with an approved immigration visa.

Requirements for Residency

* All documents submitted for this process must be originals or certified (notarized) copies
* Documents provided by the applicant must be obtained only from the responsible U.S. authorities, and authenticated by the Ecuadorian Consul
* Documents must be legally translated into Spanish if not

already in Spanish

* If you're changing visa status while in Ecuador (for example, going from a tourist visa to a resident visa) the application and associated documents must be submitted no less than 30 days prior to the expiration of the visa that you currently have

* You must register your home address with immigration authorities, and report any change of address while living in Ecuador.

All applications for resident visas require the following to be submitted:

* A visa petition addressed to the Director General of Extranjería, signed by the applicant and an attorney

* A completed form " *Solicitud de visa de inmigrante*" for the appropriate visa type

* Two notarized copies of an up-to-date passport, with the notary attesting to the fact that its status is legally current

* A completed form " *hoja de datos para la cédula*" (a data sheet, subsequently used for your identity card)

* Two current passport size photos, in color with white backdrop

* Visa fee of $350.

About the fee: These fees are current as of April 2010.

In addition to the six items above, there are additional submittals required depending on the type of visa you're asking for:

9-I: Pensioner Visa

* Retirement documents showing a stable income of at least $800 monthly, certified to be correct by the party responsible for the source of the funds, and authenticated by the Ecuadorian Consul in your country of origin
* Certification by Ecuadorian Consul that the funds are no less than $800 monthly for the applicant, plus an additional $100 for each dependent.
Note: the required income level is subject to change.

9-II: Investor of Real Estate or Securities Visa

Proof of investment of at least $25,000 (plus $500 for each dependent) demonstrated by:
* Updated certificate of title clearance indicating that there are no liens

affecting the property

* Any kind of certificates or titles, including fiduciary documents granted

by the private sector, bonds, and certificates of deposits, stocks,

and obligations

* The original and a copy of the relevant instrument, showing a term of

at least one year.

Note: This investment level is subject to change.

9-III: Industrial Investor Visa

Proof of your investment of at least $30,000.

For companies:

* Constitutive Contract or "Increase of Capital" registered at the Mercantile Registry.

For partnerships or sole proprietorships:

* Certified copy of the Commercial Registry of the corporation, or of the partnership at the Mercantile Register and at the Registro Unico de Contribuyente (RUC, Federal Tax registry)

* Business license granted by the Ministry of International Trade, Industry, and Fishing

* Agreement to comply with Article 32, numeral VII (7), of the rules and regulations determined by the Immigration Laws of Ecuador (*Ley de Extranjeria*). Consult with your nearest Consulate about this subject.

For the agricultural and/or livestock industry:

* License granted by the Ministry of International Trade, Industry, and Fishing

* Federal Tax registry (RUC)

* Property Deeds and Titles, Registered and Indemnified Membership with the Chamber of Agricultural or Chamber of the Livestock Industry

9-IV: Legal Representative, Work Visa, or Religious Visa

Legal representatives:

* General Power of Attorney specifying the representative's legal, judicial, and extrajudicial powers, registered in the *Registro Mercantil*

* The minutes from the board of shareholders meeting that

granted the Power of Attorney

* Certificate of incorporation of the company or the Amendment of Capital increase, duly registered

* Certificate of fulfillment of obligations issued by the *Superintendencia de Compañías y Bancos*, as required for each case

* Appointment as the company's legal representative, duly registered.

For persons under an Indefinite Work Contract:

* Indefinite Work Contract, legalized by the Labor Ministry

* Indefinite Work Authorization granted by the Labor Ministry.

For persons who are part of a religious organization:

* Certification which shows that the foreigner belongs to a religious

organization and states the assignment that he will be performing in

the country

* Registered appointment of the legal representative

* By-laws of the religious organization approved by the Ministerio de Gobierno.

9-V: Professional Visa

Requirements for this visa include:

* If the degree is from outside Ecuador, you must provide the original and a certified copy authenticated by the Ecuadorian Consul (in your home country), which has been validated by an accredited Ecuadorian institution of higher learning for equivalency and registered with CONESUP. The degree must be translated

* When the applicant is taking advantage of an International Agreement, a certified copy of the agreement is required

* If the degree was granted in Ecuador, provide the original and a certified copy of the degree, legalized by the granting authority and endorsed by the Ministry of Education.

9-VI: Economic Dependence Visa

The Economical Dependence Visa may be requested by an Ecuadorian citizen for his foreign spouse, children, parent, grandparent, or sibling. In addition it is granted to the family members of foreigners who have been approved for 9-I; 9-II; 9-III; 9-IV; and 9-V visas.

Applicants will need:

* The original and a certified copy of your marriage certificate. If you were married in Ecuador, this was issued by Registro Civil at the time of your marriage. If you were married outside Ecuador, the original and copy must be translated and authenticated by the Ecuadorian Consul

* If the visa is for an Ecuadorian child of non-Ecuadorian parents, you must present the *curaduría especial* and the original and copy of the child's birth certificate

* Documents that accredit the Ecuadorian nationality of the spouse, father, or mother, including their *cédula* and voting certificate. (This is not needed for those who are taking credit for another type of Immigrant visa)

* Certification of income of the applicant's sponsor

* Economical guarantee made before a notary public indicating that the sponsor will have sufficient funds for him or herself and their families to provide for their income in Ecuador. This includes the funds necessary to return to the country of origin in case it's required by authorities in Ecuador

* A copy of the sponsor's and beneficiary's passports if they are foreigners.

Non-resident Visas

If you don't want permanent residency in Ecuador, you can still remain in the country past the 90 to 180 days you'll get as a tourist. Here are the non-resident visa options available.

Student Visa, Category 12-V

Applies to: students (at all levels, regular school year) and family members accompanying the student (husband/wife, children).

Applicants will need:

* Valid passport, at least for the next six months

* Doctor's certificate and HIV test, indicating that the person does not have any communicable diseases

* Police certificate indicating that there is no record (criminal) for said person;

* Two recent photographs, passport size, in color

* School registration or proof of admission to an Ecuadorian school or institution duly recognized by the Ministry of Education

* Certificate from bank indicating good economic standing

with letter from the parent/guardian indicating that they will support the student while in Ecuador.

This visa is valid for one school year (it is not applicable for courses less than one year). It may be renewed when presenting:

* Passing grades

* Registration for the following year

* Police certificate (available in Ecuador from the police department)

* Letter of economic support.

Consular fees:

* Application: $30

* Visa: $100.

Work Visa, Category 12-VI

Applies to: Professionals of high technical levels, professionals of specialized fields, immediate family members accompanying the professional.

Applicants will need:

* Valid passport, at least for the next six months

* Doctor's certificate and HIV test, indicating that the

person does not have any communicable diseases; including HIV test

* Police certificate indicating that there is no record (criminal) for said person; two photographs

* Authorization to work, issued by the human resources office from the Ministry of Labor-duly legalized

* Copy of the working contract duly protocolized by the Ministry of Labor

* Certificate of payment to the "Instituto Ecuatoriano de Seguro Social" (Ecuadorian Social Security Office), duly authenticated by the Ministry of Foreign Affairs

* Certificate of fulfillment of requirements established by the Superintendent of Companies

* Legalized copy of the company's bylaws

* Affidavit from the hiring company or person, assuming the responsibility for expenses incurred by the foreigner as a result of abandoning the country or deportation, accompanied by the appointment, duly registered, of the legal representative-all documents duly legalized.

Valid for:

* Depends on the authorization to work from the Ministry of Labor, not exceeding two years

* General Managers, only for a year.

Consular fees:

* Application: $30

* Visa: $200.

Voluntary, Missionary, or Religious Visa, Category 12-VII

Applies to: Missionaries, volunteers, religious persons.

Applicants will need:

* *"Aplicación de Visa"* (visa application) completed and signed

* *"Certificado de Visación"* completed and signed

* Passport, valid for at least six months

* Doctor's certificate and HIV test, indicating that the person does not have any communicable diseases

* Police certificate indicating that there is no record

* Letter from legal representative of the entity requesting that the volunteer/missionary be admitted to Ecuador

* Copy of the Decree issued by the Ecuadorian government authorizing the entity to operate in Ecuador

* Copy of the appointment of the Legal representative of the

entity duly registered and authenticated by the Ministry of Foreign Affairs

* Copy of the bylaws of the host entity in Ecuador

* Affidavit from the host entity or person, assuming the responsibility for expenses incurred by the volunteer/ missionary as result of abandoning the country or deportation, duly legalized

* Affidavit from the foreigner certifying to render services at no charge

* Guarantee from the sponsoring entity to support financially the foreigner during his/her stay in Ecuador.

Valid for:

* Priests or religious missionaries, up to two years

* Lay people, up to one year.

Consular fees:

* Application: $30

* Visa: $150.

Cultural Exchange Visa, Category 12-VIII

Applies to:

* Teachers involved in cultural exchange programs (schools

in Ecuador must have bilateral agreements with schools in the U.S.)

* Students participating in cultural exchange programs

* Foreigners participating in the development of cultural exchange programs.

Applicants will need:

* *"Aplicación de Visa"* (visa application) completed and signed

* *"Certificado de Visación"* completed and signed

* Passport, valid for at least the next six months

* Doctor's certificate and HIV test, indicating that the person does not have any communicable diseases

* Police certificate indicating that there is no record

* Letter from legal representative of the sponsoring Ecuadorian entity requesting that the person be admitted to Ecuador

* Copy of the Official Registry in Ecuador, indicating the legal constitution of the entity

* Copy of the appointment of the legal representative of the entity duly registered

* Copy of the bilateral Cultural Exchange Agreement

* Affidavit from the host entity or person, assuming the

responsibility for

expenses incurred by the foreigner as result of termination of cultural exchange or deportation, duly legalized

* Affidavit from the foreigner certifying to render services at no charge. (For teachers only)

* Guarantee from the sponsoring entity to financially support the foreigner during his/her stays in Ecuador.

This visa is valid for one year.

Consular fees:

* Visa: $50

* Application: $30.

Tourist Visa, Category 12-IX

Applies to:

* Tourists

* Professional athletes

* Students

* Scientists

* Artists

* Businessmen.

Applicants will need:

* *"Aplicación de Visa"* (visa application) completed and signed

* *"Certificado de Visación"* completed and signed

* Passport, valid for at least six months

* Doctor's certificate and HIV test, indicating that the person does not have any communicable diseases.

* Police certificate indicating that there is no record

* Copy of round trip ticket to Ecuador

* Bank letter or other evidence stating that the person has good economic standing and can support himself

* Two recent photographs in color passport size.

Valid for:

* More than three and less than six months

* May be granted only once a year (as of the date the visa was granted).

Consular fees:

- Visa: $200
- Application: $30

Registering your Visa

There has been a recent change for U.S. citizens living

in Ecuador regarding registering their visas. A new *censo* card is now required by all non-Ecuadorian citizens, immigrants and non-immigrants, who hold a visa issued overseas or in Ecuador. You will not need this card if you are visiting on a tourist visa or if you do not require a visa to stay in the country. Under this new process, all visa holders will be required to go to the Ecuadorian Bureau of Immigration (*Direccion General de Extranjeria*), if you have an immigrant visa, or the Ministry of Foreign Affairs if you have a non-immigrant visa, in order to properly register your visa.

Once the visa is registered, an *orden de censo* will be issued to the applicant. To obtain this order, you must pay a fee of $4 at any branch of Banco Internacional. The final step is to go to the nearest immigration police office in the capital of your province and present the order and obtain the censocard.In Quito, offices can be found at *Alamos N 50-45 Jose Felix Barreiros* and at *Ave.*

Amazonas N32-171 y Republica.

This registration is indefinite and renewal is only required if you switch to another visa category.**Note:** This process also applies to foreigners whose visas were issued abroad

Epilogue

This book explain you how to get an Ecuadorian visa and then if you wish may get an Ecuadorian citizen. This book is writing for people that jubilate and want expend the time and money in a cheaper city like Cuenca in Ecuador.

ABOUT THE AUTHOR

I am a lawyer and my name is Freddy Quinde, I'm married and I have a beautiful daughter called Paula, my wife's name is Adriana. I was born in this city of Cuenca, and has learned to speak English in America, when I make my journey to study in a student exchange program. I am familiar with the customs of the people of Lousiana which is the State which got, the name of the school I attended was Assumpttion High school, although this did not finish my studies, I obtained the equivalent of High School from the University of New York. After a few years I was in Los Angeles where I took a course to enter university, but I continued my career in Ecuador take a doctorate in law at the Universidad del Azuay in Cuenca.